K Tables

Form Division Tables for Law

Library of Congress Classification
2010

Prepared by the Policy and Standards Division

LIBRARY OF CONGRESS
LIBRARY OF CONGRESS Cataloging Distribution Service
CONGRESS Washington, D.C.

This edition cumulates all additions and changes to the K Tables through Weekly List 2010/18, dated May 5, 2010. Additions and changes made subsequent to that date are published in weekly lists posted on the World Wide Web at

<http://www.loc.gov/aba/cataloging/classification/weeklylists/>

and are also available in *Classification Web*, the online Web-based edition of the Library of Congress Classification.

Library of Congress Cataloging-in-Publication Data

Library of Congress classification. K Tables. Form devision tables for law / prepared by the Policy and Standards Division, Library Services. — 2010 ed.
    p. cm.
"This edition cumulates all additions and changes to the K Tables through Weekly list 2010/18, dated May 5, 2010. Additions and changes made subsequent to that date are published in weekly lists posted on the World Wide Web ... and are also available in *Classification Web*, the online Web-based edition of the Library of Congress classification"— T.p. verso.
Includes index.
ISBN 978-0-8444-9509-5
1. Classification, Library of Congress. 2. Classification—Books—Law.
3. Law—Classification. I. Library of Congress. Policy and Standards Division. II. Title. III. Title: K Tables. IV. Title: Form division tables for law.

Z696.U5K78 2010
025.4'634—dc22

        2010022101

For sale by the Library of Congress Cataloging Distribution Service,
101 Independence Avenue, S.E., Washington, DC 20540-4910.
Product catalog available on the Web at **www.loc.gov/cds**.

PREFACE

The first edition *K Tables: Form Division Tables for Law* was published in 1999. Prior to that date, each individual K schedule used its own set of form division tables. Since 1999, all of the K schedules except the oldest three (KD, KE, and KF) have used this uniform set of tables, which were drafted by Jolande Goldberg, law classification specialist, and edited by Paul Weiss, senior cataloging policy specialist in the Policy and Standards Division. A 2005 edition of these tables cumulated additions and changes that were made between 1999 and 2005. This 2010 edition includes all additions and changes made since 2005.

Access to the online version of the full Library of Congress Classification is available on the World Wide Web by subscription to *Classification Web*. Details about ordering and pricing may be obtained from the Cataloging Distribution Service at:

<http://www.loc.gov/cds/>

New or revised numbers and captions are added to these tables as a result of development proposals made by the cataloging staff of the Library of Congress and cooperating institutions. Upon approval of these proposals by the weekly editorial meeting of the Policy and Standards Division, new classification records are created or existing records are revised in the master classification database. Weekly lists of newly approved or revised classification numbers and captions are posted on the World Wide Web at:

<http://www.loc.gov/aba/cataloging/classification/weeklylists/>

Kent Griffiths, assistant editor of classification schedules, is responsible for creating new classification records, maintaining the master database, and creating index terms for the captions.

Barbara B. Tillett, Chief
Policy and Standards Division

May 2010

.A15	Preliminaries. By date
	Proceedings
.A2	Indexes and tables. Digests
.A3	General. By date
.A4	Statements by participants
	Including indictments, speeches by prosecution and defense, proceedings in chambers, etc.
.A5	Evidence. By date
.A6	Judgments and minority opinions. By date
.A7	Post-trial. By date
.A8-.Z	General works on the trial. Criticism

THIS PAGE INTENTIONALLY LEFT BLANK

.xA15	Preliminaries. By date
	Proceedings
.xA2-.xA29	Indexes and tables. Digests
.xA3	General. By date
.xA4-.xA49	Statements by participants
	Including indictments, speeches by prosecution and defense, proceedings in chambers, etc.
.xA5	Evidence. By date
.xA6	Judgments and minority opinions. By date
.xA7	Post-trial. By date
.xA8-.xZ	General works on the trial. Criticism

THIS PAGE INTENTIONALLY LEFT BLANK

.A2	Collected works (Opera omnia). Selections. By date
	Including special categories of writing, e.g., observationes, quaestiones, etc.
.A3A-.A3Z	Individual works. By title, A-Z
	Including unannotated and annotated editions, translations, particular manuscript editions, and textual criticism
.A4A-.A4Z	Indexes. Repertories. Margaritae, etc., A-Z
.A5	Vocabularies. Dictionaries. By date
.A6-.Z	Biography. Criticism. Knowledge. Concept of law

THIS PAGE INTENTIONALLY LEFT BLANK

.xA2	Collected works (Opera omnia). Selections. By date
	Including special categories of writing, e.g., responsa, etc.
.xA3-.xA39	Individual works. By title
	Including unannotated and annotated editions, translations, particular manuscript editions, and including textual criticism
.xA4-.xA49	Indexes. Repertories. Margaritae, etc.
.xA5	Vocabularies. Dictionaries. By date
.xA6-.xZ	Biography. Criticism. Knowledge. Concept of law

THIS PAGE INTENTIONALLY LEFT BLANK

.A12	Collections of miscellaneous materials. By date
	Including selections of the treaty, official drafts, documents of advisory or research commissions, etc.
.A15	Indexes and tables
	Texts of, and works on, the treaty
.A2	Unannotated editions. By date
	Including official editions, with or without annotations
.A3-.Z39	Annotated editions. Commentaries. Works on the treaty
	Including private drafts
	Related agreements
	Including accessions, protocols, successions, rectifications, concessions, schedules, annexed model treaties, bilateral treaties relating to nonregional multilateral treaty, etc.
.Z4	Collections. Selections
.Z5	Individual agreements. By date of signature
	Miscellaneous documents of advisory or research commissions, etc. see K5 .A12
	Works on the treaty see K5 .A3+
.Z8	Review conferences of the parties to the treaty. By date of the conference

THIS PAGE INTENTIONALLY LEFT BLANK

.xA12	Collections of miscellaneous materials. By date
	Including selections of the treaty, official drafts, documents of advisory or research commissions, etc.
.xA15-.xA159	Indexes and tables
	Text of, and works on, the treaty
.xA2	Unannotated editions. By date
	Including official editions, with or without annotations
.xA3-.xZ39	Annotated editions. Commentaries. Works on the treaty
	Including private drafts
	Related agreements
	Including accessions, protocols, successions, rectifications, concessions, schedules, annexed model treaties, bilateral treaties relating to nonregional multilateral treaty, etc.
.xZ4	Collections. Selections. By date
.xZ5-.xZ59	Individual treaties. By country
	Subarrange by date of signature
	Miscellaneous documents of advisory or research commissions, etc. see K6 .xA12
	Works on the treaty see K6 .xA3+
.xZ8	Review conferences of the parties to the treaty. By date of the conference

THIS PAGE INTENTIONALLY LEFT BLANK

1	Bibliography
1.3	Periodicals
	Including gazettes, yearbooks, bulletins, etc.
1.5	Monographic series
	Intergovernmental congresses and conferences
	Including proceedings, reports, resolutions, final acts and works on the congress
	For other congresses, conferences, etc. see K7 4.8
2.A-Z	Congresses convened on a regular basis. By name of the congress, A-Z
	Under each:
	.xA12-.xA199 *Serials*
	.xA3 *Monographs. By date*
2.5.A-Z	Ad hoc congresses of heads of state. By name of the congress, A-Z
	Under each:
	.xA12-.xA199 *Serials*
	.xA3 *Monographs. By date*
	Treaties and other international agreements. Conventions
2.8	Indexes and tables
	Collections. Selections
	Including either multilateral or bilateral treaties, or both
3	General
3.2.A-Z	Treaties of a particular country or regional organization in the region. By country or regional organization, A-Z
3.25	Proposed treaties. Drafts (Official). Comments on drafts
3.3<date>	Multilateral treaties
	Arrange chronologically by appending the four-digit year of signature of the treaty to this number and deleting any trailing zeros. Subarrange further by Table K5
3.6.A-Z	Bilateral treaties. By country, A-Z
	Subarrange by date of signature
	For bilateral treaties between countries in the same region, see the region (e.g. Europe)
	For bilateral treaties of regional intergovernmental organizations, see the organization in the region
	For bilateral treaties relating to nonregional multilateral treaties see K7 3.3<date>
	Statutes. Statutory orders. Regulations. Directives (Legislative)
4.2	Indexes and tables. Digests
	Texts
4.3	Serials
4.4	Monographs. By date
4.45	Opinions. Recommendations
	Including consultations, target studies, etc.
	Decisions. Administrative rulings. Reports

	Decisions. Administrative rulings. Reports -- Continued
4.5	Indexes and tables. Digests. By date
4.52	Serials
4.53	Monographs. By date
4.6	Dictionaries. Encyclopedias
	Form books see K7 5
	Yearbooks see K7 1.3
4.8	Conferences. Symposia
	Including papers devoted to the scholarly exploration of a subject
4.9	Surveys on legal activities concerning unification, harmonization, cooperation, etc. Annual (official) reports
5	General works. Treatises

.A12	Bibliography
.A15	Periodicals
	Including gazettes, yearbooks, bulletins, etc.
	Monographic series see K8 .A9+
	Intergovernmental congresses and conferences
	Including proceedings, reports, resolutions, final acts, and works on the congress
	For other congresses, conferences, etc. see K8 .A6
.A2-.A29	Congresses convened on a regular basis. By name of the congress (alphabetically)

Under each:

.xA12-.xA199	*Serials*
.xA3	*Monographs. By date*

.A3-.A339	Ad hoc congresses of heads of state. By name of the congress (alphabetically)

Under each:

.xA12-.xA199	*Serials*
.xA3	*Monographs. By date*

	Treaties and other international agreements. Conventions
.A34	Indexes and tables
	Collections. Selections
	Including either multilateral or bilateral treaties, or both
.A35	General
.A37A-.A37Z	Treaties of a particular country or regional organization in the region. By country or regional organization, A-Z
.A38	Proposed treaties. Drafts (Official). Comments on drafts
.A4<date>	Multilateral treaties
	Arrange chronologically by appending the four-digit year of signature of the treaty to this number and deleting any trailing zeros. Subarrange further by Table K6
.A43A-.A43Z	Bilateral treaties. By country, A-Z
	Subarrange by date of signature
	For bilateral treaties between countries in the same region, see the region (e.g. Europe)
	For bilateral treaties of regional intergovernmental organizations, see the organization in the region
	For bilateral treaties relating to nonregional multilateral treaties see K8 .A4<date>
	Statutes. Statutory orders. Regulations. Directives (Legislative)
.A45	Indexes and tables. Digests
	Texts
.A47	Serials
.A48	Monographs. By date
.A5	Opinions. Recommendations
	Including consultations, target studies, etc.
	Decisions. Administrative rulings. Reports

	Decisions. Administrative rulings. Reports -- Continued
.A52	Indexes and tables. Digests. By date
.A53	Serials
.A54	Monographs. By date
	Dictionaries. Encyclopedias see K8 .A9+
	Form books see K8 .A9+
	Yearbooks see K8 .A15
.A6	Conferences. Symposia
.A72	Surveys on legal activities concerning unification, harmonization, cooperation, etc. Annual (official) reports
.A9-.Z9	General works. Treatises

1	Bibliography
2	Periodicals
	Including gazettes, yearbooks, bulletins, etc.
2.5	Monographic series
	Legislative documents and related works
3	Bills. By date
	Official reports. Memoranda. Records of proceedings of the legislature, etc.
	Including legislative proposals (official drafts) of the executive branch and commentaries on official drafts
3.2	Serials
3.3	Monographs. By date
	Private drafts. Criticism and comments see K9a 17
	National legislation. Federal legislation
4	Indexes and tables. Digests
	Statutes
	Collections. Selections
	Including annotated editions and commentaries
4.2	Serials
4.5	Monographs. By date
	Individual acts (or groups of acts adopted as a whole)
	Codes
	Collections. Selections see K9a 4.2+
5.5<date>	Individual codes
	Arrange chronologically by appending the four-digit year of original enactment or total revision of the code to this number and deleting any trailing zeros. Subarrange further by Table K16

	National legislation. Federal legislation
	Statutes
	Individual acts (or groups of acts adopted as a whole) -- Continued
6.5<date>	Other individual acts
	Arrange chronologically by appending the four-digit year of original enactment or total revision to this number and deleting any trailing zeros
	Under each:
	Unannotated editions
	Including official editions with or without annotations
.A3	*Serials*
.A4	*Monographs. By date*
.A6-.Z	*Annotated editions. Commentaries. General works*
	Subarrange annotated editions or commentaries by the author of the annotations or commentary, or by title if no author is designated
	For legislative documents relating to individual acts, see K9a 3+
	Comparative and uniform state, provincial, etc., legislation
	Including works comparing national, state, or provincial legislation and works comparing laws by period
	Collections. Selections
8	Unannotated editions. By date
8.4	Annotated editions. Commentaries
	Subarrange annotated editions or commentaries by the author of the annotations or commentary, or by title if no author is designated
8.6	General works
	Individual laws
	For enactments by individual states, see K9a 5.5+
9	Texts. Unannotated editions. By date
9.3	Annotated editions. Commentaries
	Subarrange annotated editions or commentaries by the author of the annotations or commentary, or by title if no author is designated
	Court decisions
9.5	Indexes and tables
10	Serials
10.3	Monographs. By date
10.5	Digests. Analytical abstracts (Leitsätze)
11	Summaries of cases

12	Dictionaries. Encyclopedias
12.2	Form books. Graphic materials
	Yearbooks see K9a 2
	Surveys of legal research see K9a 17
13.8	War and emergency legislation. By date
	Criticism. Legal reform see K9a 17
14	Conferences. Symposia
	Including papers devoted to the scholarly exploration of a subject
	Collected works (nonserial) see K9a 17
17	General works. Treatises

THIS PAGE INTENTIONALLY LEFT BLANK

1.2	Bibliography
2	Periodicals
	Including gazettes, yearbooks, bulletins, etc.
2.3	Monographic series
	Legislative documents and related works
3	Bills. By date
	Official reports. Memoranda. Records of proceedings of the legislature, etc.
	Including legislative proposals (official drafts) of the executive branch and commentaries on official drafts
3.29	Serials
3.3	Monographs. By date
	Private drafts. Criticism and comments see K9b 9
	National legislation. Federal legislation
3.5	Indexes and tables. Digests
	Statutes
	Collections. Selections
	Including annotated editions and commentaries, and including collections consisting of both statutes and regulations
3.6	Serials
4	Monographs. By date
	Individual acts (or groups of acts adopted as a whole)
	Codes
	Collections. Selections see K9b 3.6+
4.3<date>	Individual codes
	Arrange chronologically by appending the four-digit year of original enactment or total revision of the code to this number and deleting any trailing zeros. Subarrange further by Table K16

	National legislation. Federal legislation
	Statutes
	Individual acts (or groups of acts adopted as a whole) -- Continued
4.5<date>	Other individual acts
	Arrange chronologically by appending the four-digit year of original enactment or total revision to this number and deleting any trailing zeros
	Under each:
	Unannotated editions
	Including official editions with or without annotations
.A6	*Serials*
.A7	*Monographs. By date*
.A8-.Z	*Annotated editions. Commentaries. General works*
	Subarrange annotated editions or commentaries by the author of the annotations or commentary, or by title if no author is designated
	Including collections consisting of an individual act and its associated regulations
	For legislative documents relating to individual acts, see K9b 3+
	Statutory orders. Regulations. Rules of practice, etc.
	Collections. Selections
	Including annotated editions
	For collections consisting of both statutes and regulations see K9b 3.6+
	For collections consisting of an individual act and its associated regulations see K9b 4.5<date>
4.59	Serials
4.6	Monographs. By date

	Statutory orders. Regulations. Rules of practice, etc. -- Continued
4.7<date>	Individual statutory orders (or groups of regulations, etc., adopted as a whole)

Arrange chronologically by appending the four-digit year of adoption, revision, or consolidation to this number and deleting any trailing zeros

Under each:

Unannotated editions
Including official editions with or without annotations

.A19	*Serials*
.A2	*Monographs. By date*
.A5-.Z	*Annotated editions. Commentaries. General works*

Subarrange annotated editions or commentaries by the author of the annotations or commentary, or by title if no author is designated

For rules of practice before a separately classed agency, see the agency

Comparative and uniform state, provincial, etc., legislation

Including works comparing national, state, or provincial legislation and works comparing laws by period

Collections. Selections

5	Unannotated editions. By date
5.2	Annotated editions. Commentaries

Subarrange annotated editions or commentaries by the author of the annotations or commentary, or by title if no author is designated

5.3	General works

Comparative and uniform state, provincial, etc., legislation --
Continued

5.4<date> Individual laws

Arrange chronologically by appending the four-digit year of
enactment or revision of law to this number and deleting any
trailing zeros

Under each:

.A2   *Unannotated editions. By date*
Including official editions with or
without annotations

.A3-.Z   *Annotated editions. Commentaries*
Subarrange annotated editions
or commentaries by the
author of the annotations or
commentary, or by title if no
author is designated

For enactments by individual states, see K9b 4.2+

Court decisions. Reports

5.5   Indexes and tables. Digests
5.8   Serials
6   Monographs. By date

Decisions of regulatory agencies. Orders. Rulings. Reports

6.4   Serials
6.5   Monographs. By date
6.7   Digests
6.9   Indexes and tables
7.2   Dictionaries. Encyclopedias

Yearbooks see K9b 2

Criticism. Legal reform see K9b 9

7.6   Form books. Graphic materials
8   Conferences. Symposia

Including papers devoted to the scholarly exploration of a subject

Collected works (nonserial) see K9b 9

9   General works. Treatises

1	Bibliography
1.2	Periodicals
2	Monographic series
	Legislative documents and related works
3	Bills. By date
	Official reports. Memoranda. Records of proceedings of the legislature, etc.
	Including legislative proposals (Official drafts) of the executive branch and commentaries on official drafts
3.2	Serials
3.22	Monographs. By date
	National legislation. Federal legislation
3.5	Indexes and tables. Digests
	Statutes
	Collections. Selections
	Including collections consisting of both statutes and regulations
3.6	Serials. Loose-leaf editions
4	Monographs. By date
	Individual acts (or groups of acts adopted as a whole)
	Codes
	Collections. Selections see K9c 4
4.3<date>	Individual codes
	Arrange chronologically by appending the four-digit year of original enactment or total revision of the code to this number and deleting any trailing zeros. Subarrange further by Table K16
4.5<date>	Other individual acts
	Arrange chronologically by appending the four-digit year of original enactment or total revision to this number and deleting any trailing zeros
	Under each:

	.A4	*Unannotated editions. By date*
		Including official editions with or without annotations
	.A6-.Z	*Annotated editions. Commentaries. General works*
		Subarrange annotated editions or commentaries by the author of the annotations or commentary, or by title if no author is designated

Including collections consisting of an individual act and its associated regulations

For legislative documents relating to individual acts, see K9c 3+

Statutory orders. Regulations. Rules of practice, etc.

Statutory orders. Regulations. Rules of practice, etc. --
Continued
Collections. Selections
Including annotated editions
For collections consisting of both statutes and regulations
see K9c 3.6+
For collections consisting of an individual act and its
associated regulations see K9c 4.5<date>

4.6	Serials
4.7	Monographs. By date
4.8<date>	Individual statutory orders (or groups of regulations, etc., adopted as a whole)

Arrange chronologically by appending the four-digit year of
adoption, revision, or consolidation to this number and
deleting any trailing zeros
Under each:

.A2	*Unannotated editions. By date*
	Including official editions with or without annotations
.A5-.Z	*Annotated editions. Commentaries. General works*
	Subarrange annotated editions or commentaries by the author of the annotations or commentary, or by title if no author is designated

Comparative and uniform state, provincial, etc., legislation
Including works comparing federal and state legislation and works
comparing laws by period
Collections. Selections

5	Unannotated editions. By date
5.4	Annotated editions. Commentaries. General works

Subarrange annotated editions or commentaries by the author
of the annotations or commentary, or by title if no author is
designated

	Comparative and uniform state, provincial, etc., legislation -- Continued
5.7<date>	Individual laws
	Arrange chronologically by appending the four-digit year of enactment or revision of law to this number and deleting any trailing zeros
	Under each:
.A2	*Unannotated editions. By date*
	Including official editions with or without annotations
.A3-.Z	*Annotated editions. Commentaries*
	Subarrange annotated editions or commentaries by the author of the annotations or commentary, or by title if no author is designated
	For enactments by individual states, see K9c 4.192+
	Court decisions
6	Indexes and tables
6.3	Serials
6.5	Monographs. By date
6.7	Digests. Analytical abstracts
	Decisions of regulatory agencies. Orders. Rulings
6.8	Serials
6.9	Monographs. By date
7	Collections of summaries of cases decided by courts or regulatory agencies
7.3	Dictionaries. Encyclopedias
7.4	Form books. Graphic materials
	Yearbooks see K9c 1.2
	Criticism. Legal reform see K9c 10
7.7	War and emergency legislation. By date
9	Conferences. Symposia
	Including papers devoted to the scholarly exploration of a subject
	Collected works (nonserial) see K9c 10
10	General works. Treatises
	Compends. Outlines. Examination aids. Popular works see K9c 10
	Addresses, essays, lectures see K9c 10

THIS PAGE INTENTIONALLY LEFT BLANK

1	Bibliography
1.3	Periodicals
	Including gazettes, yearbooks, bulletins, etc.
1.45	Monographic series
	Legislative documents and related works
1.6	Bills. By date
	Official reports. Memoranda. Records of proceedings of the legislature, etc.
	Including legislative proposals (official drafts) of the executive branch and commentaries on official drafts
1.7	Serials
1.72	Monographs. By date
	Private drafts. Criticism and comment see K10 5.8
	National legislation. Federal legislation
2	Indexes and tables. Digests
	Statutes
	Collections. Selections
	Including annotated editions and commentaries, and including collections consisting of both statutes and regulations
2.2	Serials
2.3	Monographs. By date
2.5<date>	Individual acts (or groups of acts adopted as a whole)
	Arrange chronologically by appending the four-digit year of original enactment or total revision of the law to this number and deleting any trailing zeros
	Under each:

	Unannotated editions. By date
	Including official editions with or without annotations
.A2	*Serials*
.A4	*Monographs. By date*
.A6-.Z8	*Annotated editions. Commentaries. General works*
	Subarrange annotated editions or commentaries by the author of the annotations or commentary, or by title if no author is designated

Including enactments of national codes by individual states, etc., and including collections consisting of an individual act and its associated regulations

For legislative documents relating to individual acts, see K10 1.6+

Statutory orders. Regulations. Rules of practice, etc.

	Statutory orders. Regulations. Rules of practice, etc. -- Continued
	Collections. Selections
	Including annotated editions
	For collections consisting of both statutes and regulations see K10 2.1922+
	For collections consisting of an individual act and its associated regulations see K10 2.5<date>
3	Serials
3.3	Monographs. By date
3.45<date>	Individual statutory orders (or groups of regulations, etc., adopted as a whole)
	Arrange chronologically by appending the four-digit year of adoption, revision, or consolidation to this number and deleting any trailing zeros
	Under each:

	Unannotated editions
	Including official editions with or without annotations
.A19	*Serials*
.A2	*Monographs. By date*
.A5-.Z	*Annotated editions. Commentaries. General works*
	Subarrange annotated editions or commentaries by the author of the annotations or commentary, or by title if no author is designated

	For rules of practice before a separately classed agency, see the agency
	Comparative and uniform state, provincial, etc., legislation
	Including works comparing national, state, or provincial legislation and works comparing laws by period
	Collections. Selections
3.7	Unannotated editions. By date
3.74	Annotated editions. Commentaries
	Subarrange annotated editions or commentaries by the author of the annotations or commentary, or by title if no author is designated
3.76	General works

	Comparative and uniform state, provincial, etc., legislation -- Continued
3.8\<date\>	Individual laws

Arrange chronologically by appending the four-digit year of enactment or revision of law to this number and deleting any trailing zeros

Under each:

.A2	Unannotated editions. By date
	Including official editions with or without annotations
.A3-.Z	Annotated editions. Commentaries
	Subarrange annotated editions or commentaries by the author of the annotations or commentary, or by title if no author is designated

For enactments by individual states, see K10 2.5

	Court decisions
4	Indexes and tables. Digests
4.3	Serials
4.5	Monographs. By date
	Decisions of regulatory agencies. Orders. Rulings
4.6	Indexes and tables. Digests
4.7	Serials
4.8	Monographs. By date
4.95	Dictionaries. Encyclopedias
	Form books see K10 5.8
	Yearbooks see K10 1.3
5.3	War and emergency legislation. By date
	Criticism. Legal reform see K10 5.8
	Collected works (nonserial) see K10 5.8
5.78	Conferences. Symposia
	Including papers devoted to the scholarly exploration of a subject
5.8	General works. Treatises

THIS PAGE INTENTIONALLY LEFT BLANK

.A12	Bibliography
.A15	Periodicals
	Including gazettes, yearbooks, bulletins, etc.
	Monographic series see K11 .A15
	Legislative documents and related works
.A2	Bills. By date
	Official reports. Memoranda. Records of proceedings of the legislature, etc.
	Including legislative proposals (official drafts) of the executive branch and commentaries on official drafts
.A22	Serials
.A23	Monographs. By date
	Private drafts. Criticism and comment see K11 .A9+
	National legislation. Federal legislation
.A25	Indexes and tables. Digests
	Statutes
	Collections. Selections
	Including annotated editions and commentaries, and including collections consisting of both statutes and regulations
.A27	Serials. Loose-leaf editions
.A28	Monographs. By date
.A31<date>	Individual acts (or groups of acts adopted as a whole)

        Arrange chronologically by appending the four-digit year of original enactment or total revision of the law to this number and deleting any trailing zeros

        Under each:

	Unannotated editions
	Including official editions with or without annotations
.xA2-.xA29	*Serials*
.xA4	*Monographs. By date*
.xA6-.xZ8	*Annotated editions. Commentaries. General works*
	Subarrange annotated editions or commentaries by the author of the annotations or commentary, or by title if no author is designated

        Including enactments of national codes by individual states, etc., and including collections consisting of an individual act and its associated regulations

        For legislative documents relating to individual acts, see K11 .A2+

    Statutory orders. Regulations. Rules of practice, etc.

        For rules of practice before a separately classed agency, see the issuing agency

Statutory orders. Regulations. Rules of practice, etc. --
Continued
Collections. Compilations
For collections consisting of both statues and regulations
see K11 .A27+
For collections consisting of an individual act and its
associated regulations see K11 .A31<date>
.A32   Serials. Loose-leaf editions
.A33   Monographs. By date
.A35<date>   Individual statutory orders, etc. (or groups of statutory orders,
etc. adopted as a whole)
Arrange chronologically by appending the four-digit year of
original adoption or revision of the statutory order, etc. to this
number and deleting any trailing zeros
Under each:

	Texts. Unannotated editions
	Including official editions with or
	without annotations
.xA2-.xA29	*Serials*
.xA4	*Monographs. By date*
.xA6-.xZ8	*Annotated editions. Commentaries.*
	General works
	Subarrange annotated editions
	or commentaries by the
	author of the annotations or
	commentary, or by title if no
	author is designated

Comparative and uniform state, provincial, etc. legislation
Including works comparing national, state, or provincial legislation
and works comparing laws by period
.A4   Unannotated editions. By date
.A46   Annotated editions. Commentaries. General works
Subarrange annotated editions or commentaries by the author of
the annotations or commentary, or by title if no author is
designated
Court decisions and related materials. Reports
Including decisions of quasi-judicial (regulatory) agencies
.A473   Indexes and tables. Digests
.A48   Serials
.A49   Monographs. By date
Decisions of regulatory agencies. Orders. Rulings see K11
.A47+
Dictionaries. Encyclopedias see K11 .A9+
Form books see K11 .A9+
Yearbooks see K11 .A15
Criticism. Legal reform see K11 .A9+

	Collected works (nonserial) see K11 .A9+
.A67	Conferences. Symposia
	Including papers devoted to the scholarly exploration of a subject
.A9-.Z9	General works. Treatises

THIS PAGE INTENTIONALLY LEFT BLANK

.xA15-.xA199	Periodicals
	Including official gazettes, yearbooks, bulletins, etc.
.xA2	Legislative documents. Working documents. Official reports. By date
	Treaties. Statutes. Statutory orders (Collective or individual). Rules
.xA29-.xA299	Serials
.xA3	Monographs. By date
	Cases. Decisions (Collective or individual). Measures. Opinions
.xA5-.xA519	Serials
.xA52	Monographs. By date
.xA7-.xZ9	General works. Treatises

THIS PAGE INTENTIONALLY LEFT BLANK

1.2	Bibliography
1.3	Periodicals
	Including gazettes, yearbooks, bulletins, etc.
1.5	Monographic series
	Treaties and other international agreements. Conventions
2	Indexes and tables
3	Collections. Selections
	Including either multilateral or bilateral treaties, or both
3.2	Proposed treaties. Drafts (Official). Comments on drafts. By date
3.3<date>	Multilateral treaties
	Arrange chronologically by appending the four-digit year of signature of the treaty to this number and deleting any trailing zeros. Subarrange further by Table K5
3.5.A-Z	Bilateral treaties
	Subarrange by date of signature
	For bilateral treaties relating to multilateral treaties see K13 3.3<date>
	Other official acts and legal measures
	Regulations and decisions
3.6	Indexes and tables
3.8	Abridgments and digests
	Collections. Selections
	Including annotated editions
4	Serials
4.2	Monographs. By date

Other official acts and legal measures

Regulations and decisions -- Continued

4.3<date> Individual acts (or groups of acts adopted as a whole)

Arrange chronologically by appending the four-digit year of original enactment or revision of the law to this number and deleting any trailing zeros

Under each:

.A15	*Indexes and tables*
	Legislative documents and related works
.A2	*Collections. Selections. By date*
.A3	*Drafts (Official). By date*
.A32	*Records of proceedings. Minutes of evidence, reports, etc., of the organ and its committees. By date*
	For annual (official) reports, see "Surveys on legal activity concerning unification, harmonization, cooperation. Annual (official) reports," below
.A4	*Miscellaneous documents. By date*
	Including memoranda, documents of fact-finding, advisory, research, or drafting committees, etc.
	Unannotated editions
	Including official editions with or without annotation
.A5	*Serials*
.A6	*Monographs. By date*
.A7-.Z	*Annotated editions. Commentaries. General works*
	Subarrange annotated editions or commentaries by the author of the annotations or commentary, or by title if no author is designated

4.4 Recommendations. Opinions

Including action programs, consultations, target studies, etc.

Administrative decisions. Reports

4.5 Indexes and tables

4.52 Serials

4.53 Monographs. By date

4.6 Court decisions and related materials. Reports

4.8	Surveys on legal activity concerning unification, harmonization, cooperation. Annual (official) reports
4.85	Dictionaries. Encyclopedias
	Form books see K13 5
4.95	Conferences. Symposia
	Including papers devoted to the scholarly exploration of a subject
5	General works. Treatises

THIS PAGE INTENTIONALLY LEFT BLANK

.A12	Bibliography
.A15	Periodicals
	Including gazettes, yearbooks, bulletins, etc.
	Monographic series see K14 .A9+
	Treaties and other international agreements. Conventions
.A2	Indexes and tables
.A23	Collections. Selections
	Including either multilateral or bilateral treaties, or both
.A28	Proposed treaties. Drafts (official). Comments on drafts. By date
.A3<date>	Multilateral treaties
	Arrange chronologically by appending the four-digit year of signature of the treaty to this number and deleting any trailing zeros. Subarrange further by Table K6
.A34A-.A34Z	Bilateral treaties. By country, A-Z
	Subarrange by date of signature
	For bilateral treaties relating to multilateral treaties see K14 .A3<date>
	Other official acts and legal measures
	Regulations and decisions
.A36	Indexes and tables
.A38	Abridgments and digests
	Collections. Selections
	Including annotated editions
.A4	Serials
.A42	Monographs. By date

	Other official acts and legal measures
	Regulations and decisions -- Continued
.A43\<date>	Individual acts (or groups of acts adopted as a whole)

Arrange chronologically by appending the four-digit year of original enactment or revision of the law to this number and deleting any trailing zeros

Under each:

.xA2	*Working documents. Official records. By date*
	Including reports and memoranda of factfinding, advisory, research, and drafting committees, etc., and drafts
.xA7	*Unannotated editions. By date*
	Including official editions with or without annotation
.xA8-.xZ8	*Annotated editions. Commentaries. General works*
	Subarrange annotated editions or commentaries by the author of the annotations or commentary, or by title if no author is designated

.A5	Opinions. Recommendations
	Including action programs, consultations, target studies, etc.
	Administrative decisions see K14 .A9+
.A7	Court decisions and related materials. Reports
.A72	Surveys on legal activity concerning unification, harmonization, cooperation. Annual (official) reports
.A8	Conferences. Symposia
	Including papers devoted to the scholarly exploration of a subject
.A9-.Z9	General works. Treatises

.A12	Bibliography
.A15	Periodicals
	Including gazettes, yearbooks, bulletins, etc.
.A18	Treaties and rules governing the organization. By date
	Working documents. Official records
	Including research publications
.A3	Indexes and tables. Digests
	For indexes and tables to a particular publication, see the publication
.A35	Rules of order. Rules of procedure
	Records of proceedings of the organ and its committees, etc.
.A4	Serials
.A45	Monographs. By date
	Decisions. Measures. Resolutions. Recommendations
	Including opinions, consultations, etc.
.A47	Indexes and tables. Digests
	Collections. Selections
.A5	Serials
.A6	Monographs. By date
	Individual
	see the subject
.A7	Surveys on legal activities. Annual (Official) reports
	Yearbooks see K15 .A15
.A9-.Z9	General works on the organ, commission, etc.

THIS PAGE INTENTIONALLY LEFT BLANK

.A12   Indexes and tables
                            Legislative documents and related works
.A14   Bills. By date
                                    Including records of proceedings and minutes of evidence
.A32   Documents of code commissions and revision commissions.
                                    Official reports. Memoranda. By date
                                        Including legislative proposals (Official drafts) of the executive
                                            branch and commentaries on drafts
                                Private drafts. Contemporary criticism and comment on private
                                    drafts see K16 .A6+
.A52   Text of the code. Unannotated editions. By date
                                    Including official editions with or without annotations, and works
                                        containing the introductory act and complementary legislation
                                        together with the text of the code
                                    For individual complementary laws, see the subject
.A6-.Z8   Annotated editions. Commentaries. General works
                                    Subarrange annotated editions or commentaries by the author of
                                        the annotations or commentary, or by title if no author is
                                        designated
.Z9   Amendatory laws. By date of enactment
                                    For amendatory laws pertaining to a particular subject, see the
                                        subject

THIS PAGE INTENTIONALLY LEFT BLANK

.A18	Documents of revision commissions. By date
.A2	Constitutional conventions
	Including proceedings, debates, etc.
.A3	Preliminary drafts of new constitution. By date
	Private drafts. Proposed constitutions. Contemporary criticism and comment see K17 .A7+
.A5	Works on the legislative history (origin and making) of the constitution
	Text of the constitution
.A6	Unannotated editions. By date
	Including official editions, annotated and unannotated
.A7-.Z5	Annotated editions. Commentaries. General works
	Subarrange annotated editions or commentaries by the author of the annotations or commentary, or by title if no author is designated
.Z8	Amendments. Proposed amendments. By date of publication or rejection
.Z9	Constitution compared with other constitutions

THIS PAGE INTENTIONALLY LEFT BLANK

	Reports
.A2	Serials
.A3	Monographs. By date
.A4-.Z6	Digests. Summaries
.Z7	Citators. Tables of cases overruled, etc.
.Z8	Indexes and tables
	For indexes and other finding aids related to a particular publication, see the publication
.Z9	Records and briefs

THIS PAGE INTENTIONALLY LEFT BLANK

.A2   Indexes and tables
                                Including general and comprehensive indexes, and indexes to
                                    decisions published in law journals
                                For indexes relating to a particular collection, see the publication
                        General collections. Selections
.A35   Serials
.A4   Monographs. By date
.A7-.Z   Summaries of judgments. Analytical abstracts

THIS PAGE INTENTIONALLY LEFT BLANK

Text
> Including unannotated and annotated editions, facsimiles, or originals; and including typographical reproductions of the text entirely in non-Roman or ancient type, or transliterated in Roman characters

2.2	Entire work. By date
	Including bilingual editions
2.22.A-Z	Individual parts or sections. Selections. By title, A-Z
	Including fragments and epitomes (abridgments) and bilingual editions
3.A-Z	Particular manuscript editions. By title or location, A-Z
	Including editions of entire work as well as parts and sections
6.A-Z	Translations. Paraphrases in other languages (without edition of original text). By language, A-Z, and date
	Including entire work, sections, or selections
6.5	Indexes. Chronologies. Concordances
7	General works. Textual criticism. Controversy

> Class here modern works on the source, including interpolation technique, exegetics, etc.
> For epigraphy and papyrology, see KJA190 ; KL190 ; and KQ190
> For philological studies, see PJ

THIS PAGE INTENTIONALLY LEFT BLANK

	Text. Unannotated and annotated editions
	Including facsimiles or originals; and including typographical reproductions of the text entirely in non-Roman or ancient type, or transliterated in Roman characters
.A2	Entire work. By date of edition
	Including bilingual editions
.A22A-.A22Z	Individual parts or sections. Selections. By title, A-Z
	Including fragments and epitomes (abridgments) and bilingual editions
.A3A-.A3Z	Particular manuscript editions. By title or location, A-Z
	Including editions of entire work as well as parts or sections
.A4A-.A4Z	Translations. Paraphrases in other languages (without edition of original text). By language, A-Z, and date
	Including entire work, sections, or selections
.A5	Vocabularies. Dictionaries. By date
.A6	Indexes. Chronologies. Concordances
.A8-.Z	General works on the source. Textual criticism. Controversy
	Including monographic-systematic comment on the source, interpolation technique, etc., and including early (contemporary) works
	For epigraphy and papyrology, see KBR190 ; KJA190 ; KL190 ; KQ190
	For philological studies, see PJ

THIS PAGE INTENTIONALLY LEFT BLANK

	Text. Unannotated editions
	Including modernized versions
0.2	Entire work. By date
0.22.A-Z	Individual parts or sections. By title, A-Z
0.3.A-Z	Particular manuscript editions. By title or location, A-Z
	Including editions of entire work as well as parts or sections
	Iconography. Bilderhandschriften
0.4.A-Z	Individual. By title or location, A-Z
0.44.A-Z	Collections of illuminations from manuscripts and printed works. By editor, compiler, or title, A-Z
	Glosses. Commentaries. Annotated editions
0.5.A-Z	Entire work. By annotator, editor, commentator, or title
0.52.A-Z	Individual parts. By annotator, editor, commentator, or title
0.55.A-Z	Individual sections. By annotator, editor, commentator, or title
0.6.A-Z	Translations. Paraphrases in other languages (without edition of original text). By language, A-Z, and date
0.7	General works on the source. Textual criticism. Controversy
	Including monographic-systematic comment on the source
	For early (contemporary) works see K20c 0.5+
0.8.A-Z	Special topics, A-Z

THIS PAGE INTENTIONALLY LEFT BLANK

	Text. Unannotated and annotated editions
	Including facsimiles or originals; and including typographical reproductions of the text entirely in non-Roman or ancient type, or transliterated in Roman characters; and including bilingual editions
.xA2	Entire work. By date
.xA22	Individual parts or sections. Selections. By date
.xA3-.xA399	Particular manuscript editions. By title or location
	Including editions of the entire work as well as parts or sections
.xA4	Translations. Paraphrases in other languages (without edition of original text). By date
	Including entire work, sections, or selections
.xA5	Vocabularies. Dictionaries. By date
.xA6	Indexes. Chronologies. Concordances
.xA8-.xZ	General works on the source. Textual criticism. Controversy
	Including monographic-systematic comment on the source, interpolation technique, etc., and including early (contemporary) works
	For philological studies, see PJ

THIS PAGE INTENTIONALLY LEFT BLANK

	Statutes. Regulations. Privileges. Custumals. Treaties, etc.
.A2	Collections. Selections
.A4	Individual laws
	Including unannotated and annotated editions (Glosses)
.A55	Court decisions. Dooms. Advisory opinions
.A7-.Z79	General works. Treatises

THIS PAGE INTENTIONALLY LEFT BLANK

	The numbers <1>-<4> are provided in this table as an alternative arrangement for libraries using this classification. At the Library of Congress, the material indicated by these numbers is classed in JZ
<1>	General collections
	Foreign relations and diplomatic correspondence
	Secretary of State, Minister of Foreign Affairs
<2>	Reports. Memoranda. Correspondence
	Including bureau reports and documents, press releases, etc.
	Diplomatic correspondence
	Class here general collections, routine correspondence, etc.
	Cf. Classes D, E, F, etc. for correspondence covering special affairs, negotiations, wars, etc.
<3>	Serials
<3.5>	Indexes. Lists of documents, etc.
<3.52>	Relations with particular countries
	see the country in classes D - F
<4>	General legislative papers. By date
	Including Senate (Upper house), House (Lower house), and other
	General administrative and executive papers
	see subclass J
	Digests of decisions, opinions, etc. see K23 7.7
	Treaties and conventions
5	Indexes. Registers
	Collections
5.3	Serials
	Including official and non-official
6	Monographs. By date
7	Individual treaties. By date of signature
	Subarrange further by Table K5
	Indexes. Registers see K23 5
7.7	Digests of decisions. Opinions, etc.
8	Cases, claims, etc.
	All cases and claims to which the United States or a US citizen is a party are classed in KZ238+
8.A2	General collections
8.A4-Z	By name of plaintiff nation, A-Z
9	By date
	Including private claims
10.A-Z	States, provinces, departments, etc., A-Z
	Class here source materials from states, provinces, departments, or other subordinate jurisdictions that were formerly autonomous and maintained independent foreign relations, treaty rights, etc.

THIS PAGE INTENTIONALLY LEFT BLANK

	The numbers <.A1>-<.A5> are provided in this table as an alternative arrangement for libraries using this classification. At the Library of Congress, the material indicated by these numbers is classed in JZ
<.A1-.A19>	General collections
	Foreign relations and diplomatic correspondence
	Secretary of State, Minister of Foreign Affairs
<.A2-.A29>	Reports. Memoranda
	Including bureau reports and documents, press releases, etc.
<.A3>	Diplomatic correspondence
	Class here general collections, routine correspondence, etc.
	Cf. Classes D, E, F, etc. for correspondence covering special affairs, negotiations, wars, etc.
<.A4-.A48>	General legislative papers
	Including Senate (Upper house), House (Lower house), and other
<.A5>	General administrative and executive papers
	Treaties and conventions
	Indexes. Registers see K24 .A75
	Collections
.A58	Serials
	Including official and non-official
.A6	Monographs. By date
.A7	Individual treaties. By date of signature
	Subarrange further by Table K6
.A75	Indexes. Registers
	Cases, claims, etc.
	Claims and arbitration cases are entered under defendant nation, and subarranged by name of the plaintiff nation. Group claims are entered by plaintiff nation. Cases and claims to which the United States or a US citizen is a party are classed in KZ238+
.A82	General collections
.A84A-.A84Z	By name, A-Z
.A85	By date
.A9-.Z	States, provinces, departments, etc., A-Z
	Class here source materials from states, provinces, departments, or other subordinate jurisdictions that were formerly autonomous and maintained independent foreign relations, treaty rights, etc.

GPO　U.S. GOVERNMENT PRINTING OFFICE: 2010–357–308/40005

NOTES

NOTES

NOTES

NOTES

NOTES

NOTES

NOTES

NOTES